ONE BRIGHT AND REAL CARESS

Poems

Ryan Van Lenning

Book 2 in the *Re-Membering* Series

Copyright © 2025
by Wild Nature Heart Press

All rights reserved.
Use of this material with attribution is welcome.

For inquires, contact
ryan@wildnatureheart.com

Cover Design by cover hub

ISBN: 978-1-7368776-6-1

WildNatureHeart.com

For the moment...

CONTENTS

INTRODUCTION	1
NOW MEANS NOW	2
A Buried Yes	3
With Such Hands As These	4
1000 Ways and One	5
How to Celebrate (Start With a Frog)	7
Now Means Now	9
Feet In Sand, Head In Water	10
What Would Be a Hello?	12
Bewildered and Blessed	13
Atopia	14
Insta-Season	16
LIFE'S PARTNER	18
Tender Intervals In This Perpetual Departure	19
At the Feet of That Brutal, Beloved Teacher	21
The Treasure at the Bottom of Each Breath	23
Song of the Old Skull	24
Rave On Bold Scratchers	26
I'M IN IT FOR GOOD, I PROMISE	27
By Invitation Only	28
Set an Altar Upon the Sun	30
Record of Life	31
Always Here	32
I Bent My Ear	34
She Saunters Ripe With the Season	35
Persimmon	36
Boann	37

I, TOO, AM LARGE, CONTAINING MULTITUDES	40
The Great Affirmation: Well-Stretched Arms	41
The Great Affirmation: Glad of My Paws	44
The Great Affirmation: Vast Arousal	46
The Great Affirmation: Petty Heart, Beautiful Heart	49
THIS MESSY CELEBRATION	51
Savage Pulse	52
This Messy Celebration	54
Trust the Shimmerings	56
That Hole in the Horizon	58
Sirening	60
Freckle	62
ONLY IN IT FOR THE CONVERGENCE	64
Tell Me, Where Do You Mark the Center?	65
Don't Puzzle Over the Meaning	68
The Waves Know	70
Memoir: All the Holy Things	73
About the Author	76
About Wild Nature Heart	77
Other Titles in the *Re-Membering Series*	78
Excerpts From Ryan Van Lenning's forthcoming books	81

INTRODUCTION

Build an altar at each moment with a goodbye on the tip of the tongue.

Slow dance drunk in the robust now.

Show up with playful paws and the gravity of worms.

Strap the searchlight around your ribs and shuffle like a crescent moon over all your little resistances.

Saunter past all the gates.

Slit yourself down the middle, pull your skin to the horizon and
drip like a mountain.

Can we be here now?

These are some of the invitations lurking in the 40 poems of *One Bright and Real Caress*. This collection is a celebration of the moment. Of not escaping. Of impermanence. Of death as life partner.

With syllables of relentless affirmation, these poems bring an unconditional caress over all the textures of life and our multitudes within. As an invitation to presence and an honoring of the all-too-real struggle to not flee the moment, *One Bright and Real Caress* welcomes every conceivable crescent mood, slivered and slow, with no aim but to edge out more and more into the whole ceremony and celebration.

So again: *Can we be here now? Really be here?*

NOW MEANS NOW

A Buried Yes

with what mounds of dirt and detritus
with what concrete callous regard
are all these yearning Yeses lost?

Oh, world, you ask for Holy Yeses.

You say, "Unbury the Ark of Ancient Affirmations."

So, I, a dutiful servant, pick up
my sacred shovel
and begin the dirt-digging devotion.

With Such Hands As These

With such hands as these,
fear finds no place
to plant its dark seed.

The moon...
the sun....
the waves...
wash over and into us.

Wind offers her gentle balms
and green rests assured.

Tomorrow and a million tomorrows
will still be here caressing the world—
we have deep time on our side.

1000 Ways and One

I've got 1000 ways to leave my heart–
Some are named
others aren't

A 1000 ways to flee the scene–
none of which
make me free

A 1000 routes to resist what is–
skip the season,
jump ahead

A 1000 paths from heart to head–
my body left for dead

A 1000 claws to cling to pain–
keep it close,
push trust away

A 1000 strategies of escape–
no matter what
shape it takes

A 1000 forms of being right–
a sharpness
urging flight or fight

A 1000 paths to plot and prey–
make sure things
go my way

But there's just one way

I've found to stay

it wears the face
of pause and play

like these streams of sun right now
traveling through creative clouds

Falling on the field within
welcoming what is, and then,

Feeds the wonder, finds the Wow
frees the beauty, fuels the bow

Restores me to the Sacred Why
Anchors me in biggest skies

Returns me to the many hearts–
Some are named,
others aren't

How to Celebrate (Start With a Frog)

Start with a frog.

In the mud by the shore
the day begins.

In the sky by the hawk, or
inside the stones under water.

Whatever word they use to mean
how morning's light
bursts open on low rapids—use it here.

Tell me, how did the day smile
from each corner of its face?

With glee and fire.

Oh, if you were a builder, you'd place
an altar at each place.

But the thing about Now—
no monuments serve better
than your presence.

How to praise:
Open your hands and find a sun—
all the sand will pour out

along with all the sighs
you'd been gathering for ages
joining the other out-breaths
of a summer flow.

You swear you're not a hoarder
but the frog is not convinced

and says keep hopping and let it go.

Without trying, you touch everything
and everything touches you:

pampas grass and salmon
wild mustard and wild moons
poison oak becoming guardian oak
more red than red alder leaves
and busy flickers white-banded and belling
into the wind

and of course those frogs
delicate and intrepid.

When you hitch your beautiful note
to the river-chord
after all these eons,
finally, the heron believes you.

So, picking a paw full of berries to celebrate—
one for each moment of the morning—
stain yourself
the deep color of joy.

Now Means Now

With each shimmering golden wing
each leaf aloft on autumn wind

then dropped to ground in crimson flight
in the season's sinking light

like confessions of an ancient tree
whispering longings to be free

each dragonfly, hovered, huddled
and river's curled lip is uttered

silver across the stones at dusk
and fall climbs out its summer husk

with each merganser's arrowed head
bobbing towards the western shore

a ripple races back and forth
across the water, and even more

it enters and somehow endows me
with a never-ending singing "Wow,

it's now and now, and now!"

Feet In Sand, Head In Water
For Theodore Roethke

The slide of slick unrest
poking its fingers in my eye.

It's over there, it said.
Somewhere, something else, not here, not this.

Those fingers, they're mine. I grew them day by day.

Fill me with deep regard,
was the voice meeting it
from somewhere within the ribs.

A holy hunger abides. Toes wiggle
the mind.

Once more raised to lips, to eye, once more
into inveterate stomach,
from wayward heart,
once more…

anything but now, here.

Away, flying again
from the staying.

You want the Now, you say, it said.
But won't stay.

A lie.

No, not lying, feeble and ignorant.

It's hard to be now.

What more do you want?

No, not hard. Here. Nothing else.

Ok, try again.

Taking my fingers out...
Feet in sand, water in mind.

What Would Be a Hello?

What would be a hello,
and what would be getting lost
in the labyrinth?

To greet and say hello—
unguarded, curious
but not agenda-ed.

Bereft of ceremony,
but not without elegance.

Hello with the belly, hi with the eyes.
Not moving, but meeting and receiving.

Not stepping out of the sun,
nor out of the shadow,

To greet and be greeted
without a word, without award.

But not without reward.

What would be tasting the fruit
and what would be a trap door?

In vast rippled silence,
a hello from the big sky within?

The wind enjoys seeing that.

Just enough to begin.

Bewildered and Blessed

Pour tradition into these tendril moments
letting them climb up
the bean pole of you

In this vast experiment
of remembering

Welcoming every conceivable
crescent mood, slivered and slow

with no aim but to edge out
more and more
for the whole ceremony
and celebration

Thank you thank you
Deliverer of Death

The bow of a thousand radiant moons to you
Doorway to Desire

Thank you for taking us home

Showing us where life was lost
and loss let life

When we, errant wanderers,
who once begged for seats
at the table of belonging

finally unflex our fingers
hoarding moon and magic

finally relinquish all proving
and sit down, bewildered and blessed.

Atopia

There you go again
half way to somewhere else

which is a somewhere
that you'll also try to flee

without really being there
with the tidal fog
and stinging nettles of you

one foot out of the door
of the moment

allergic to the shelter-in-
the-here-and-now

and its ravine of awe-full voices

On the other hand–
on which there are at least five
more ways of touching things–
Perhaps no place

is exactly where you need to be
for the strange and slick surprise to unfold

Without some tight agenda
some do-gooder-grasping
for a spring on the other side
on which you really belong

Perhaps it's no u-
nor -dys place

but -a no place

the deepest center
of everywhere and when
inside which your breath is found

But how to get from there
to the next season of things
is anybody's guess

even the nettle seed
and tidal fog
and the ravine that holds them all

Insta-Season

Press 1 for Autumn

You work hard,
you deserve crisp air
and a pile of colored leaves.

Why wait? Order your season today
The more you buy, the more you save.

Press 2 to fast forward to spring
if the orange is too bright
and evenings too dark and chill.

Do you long for lilies?

Why be satisfied with the pace
of Earth?

Why be satisfied with November nights
when you are feeling like first of May?
Spring can be yours today.
Don't wait, don't delay!

New and Improved!
Summer, now organic and free range
with zero calories.

Get yours now!

Tired of waiting for the sun?
Press 3 to get rid of that winter body
and slim into summer.

Miss that cozy-by-the-fire feel
and smell?

Press 4 to have winter vibes
delivered to your door.

With Insta-Season,
you don't have to be chained
to the seasons.

Have the sun delivered right to your door
inbox/sensory input system
in no time.

(Check your spam folder if you haven't received it)

First-time callers receive
a simulated wind-packet,
your very own pocket fan.

Feel the breeze on your skin
when and how you want it

You're in control!
(AAA-batteries not included)

Free shipping and handling on orders
of over three elements.

Thank you for your order—
your product will arrive in three minutes.

**Free gift if you order now, for a limited time only:

Your own personalized moon
injection-molded with colored plastic
and engraved with your very own initials.
Keep your moon inside with you
so you never have to go outside.

LIFE'S PARTNER

Tender Intervals In This Perpetual Departure

If it's not you with one foot out
the door of the moment

It's the moment ever fleeing itself
afraid of its own center

How we disappear when we disappear ourselves—
we live nowhere
fleeing all the time

Never arriving
until the final midnight
when old hair and new petals alike
become dust

as all the fine fragrances fade
even if they never found a nose

How so many of the species of our love
don't make the endangered list
until after they've gone extinct

That last lover's touch before
the doings of the day

And it's always the last touch,
says the sun sliding into the sea

How the child in us wants
whatever it can't have
and rejects what's right in front of it.

Even the thought-we-knews
and all the familiar hearts
so soon take leave

and memory walks around
like a ghost

stirring up the scattered wind
once in a while

How even now, when spring barges in
with its thousand clarion calls
and comings-out

one hears the sound of leaves
dropping on the other side
all the goings-under

No, we don't want to hear it—
How everything is perpetual departure.

But we, the fragile ones, we live
for the tender intervals
thin as new feathers

And perhaps if we're lucky,
we can bring one bright and real caress
to the thing

(The title is taken from
a line in Rilke's French poem *Les Roses*)

At the Feet of That Brutal, Beloved Teacher

What does it mean to walk with death?

You can walk with death
as an act of imagination
having conversations with love
on the way to the death lodge

Don't think it's not there
just because you made it up

You can walk with death
as an uninvited guest
climbing hand over fist
with a closed throat
up the mountain

You can make of yourself an apprentice
at the feet of that brutal, beloved teacher
learning lessons sorely needed

knowing that fall lives in the spring seed.

For how can you really be here
saying hello to each moment
without a goodbye
on the tip of your tongue?

That is how to pray, it says,
the first and only lesson.

Finally, you can walk with death
as life's partner
hand in hand, allied
like a ripe citizen of the earth

with, if not praise, then respect
holding it gently to your heart

for this one who arrives at every hour
or any hour

So do not be surprised
by its walking onto the scene
with a beguiling smile

Praise will come later
when the heart swells beyond measure

For is that not the way
of each bright new petal

every astonishing sunset
taking your breath away?

Taking away all breaths
so there may be the new?

The Treasure at the Bottom of Each Breath

The old way of holding things
sank into the sea
with the diving god
and sprouted dawnwings
as an owl flying out of one hand

gentle dawnfingers
caressing Earth with the other

with my mycelium strung between
finding nutrients in everything

I barely had a chance to say goodbye
to the old way

Before the way to say goodbye
became the treasure
at the bottom of each breath and day
the bottom of each moment's play

Which was also how to pray hello
and mean it

like one of the great lovers
of the world

Without fists or fortresses
and nothing but a Cosmos to call home

Song of the Old Skull

They didn't teach this in school—
that we all live inside
the song of the old skull

the one found in every desert wash
and forest den

rippling across entire continents
of confusions and certainties

how every wind
touches every other wind

how it requires many seasons
to shape your true form

how even the teachers can't teach—
you have to find out yourself

Part of an seemingly impossible curriculum
called 'how to be here'

with lesson plans
on how to say goodbye

how the song sounds different
to different ears

a chant, an unintentional prayer
a grave drone, a shriek.

How if you pick up its melody
a string of fat notes can calm you

or send you evaporating

but it's the same thing

how its chorus thrums salvation
grrrunka...grrrunka...grrrunka

however it's heard
you'll always be inside it

holding you like sky holds the moon
and the moon holds the brutal loving sun

who bakes the strange fangs
that pierce every thick moment

Rave On Bold Scratchers

Stretch big and rave on bold scratchers.

Stretch out towards the world
pouring into you

trying to capture the
endless bouquets of beauty and pain

Scratch black and white shapes
and florid brushstrokes
on all your canvasses

Conjure melodies
like raving magicians

all the while knowing
we're mere clouds blowing through,
transient guests on vacation.

Like everything.

One day we'll sit with the final sunset
with only the merest scratch
in the sand remaining

and even that will be
reclaimed by the great sea
at midnight–
just as we will be.

Yet still we stretch and scratch.

We are alive.

Stretch big and rave on bold scratchers.

I'M IN IT FOR GOOD, I PROMISE

By Invitation Only

Everybody is here by invitation only.

In these parts she's the host.

The Great River, whose ears
are never closed,
hears autumn knock gently
with mottled wings of crimson-gold
on her front porch.

But I find myself on the back porch
and fall doesn't even notice me.

Here at the party,
there are no mutters or stutters
though when I've filled myself
with all the wrong things
that's all I can manage.

I'm no good at small talk,
but I can't abide my own snapping shut,
my own slinking away—

so I'll sit and listen, I say...I plead...
to somebody who has ears
and eyes, but no face.

Or rather, infinite faces.

Now I'm in it for good, I promise.

I've made the promises
it'll kill me not to keep,
but it nearly kills me to keep them

the way season nearly sinks the sun
and green
in its fabulous dream.

I fall asleep.

But this time, THIS time, I'll open everything,
I whisper to myself,
braving the light
streaming through the door.

I'll open everything. (Did I say that out loud?)

Yes, even the bolts rusting
on the hinges of my hidden doors
will come out.

Because she hears everything
she just grins her welcome grin
and carries on,
the life of the party.

And I step in to join.

I'm in it for good, I promise.

Set an Altar Upon the Sun

Set an altar upon the sun
Red ripe and fingers three
Leaves of love and veined they run
on the magic maple tree

Stretch to fetch an outer one
to see what's seldom seen
Or fan the leaves just for fun
to break your season free

Record of Life

If you use your nights
to forget your days

but then forget to write
your days

where will the record
of your life be kept?

Take leave of nights long-looted
and amnesiac days so muted

and make a monument
of each moment

not by some big gesture
but by letting spacious hellos
spill out of you

Let open skies
pour through you like seawater
through endless fingers

then you will be the pen
and the paper

the indelible ink

in the mysterious book
that flies off the shelf
haunted whole with life

Always Here

Why did you bring me here?
You are always here

at the beautiful cusp
of expansion and contraction

Yes, but Why did you bring me here?
Why did *we* bring *us* here?

You see, it's all the Sea—
River, I trust your journey

What Preposterous Pulse pretending
to be a me

What Preposterous Pulse pretending
to be a you

How will you show up?
With dust on my feet

How will you show up?
With scratches on my skin

How will you show up?
With fennel on my breath

How will you show up?
With Ocean in my eyes

How will you show up?
Shoulder to the Wheel

How will you show up?
With playful paws

How will you show up?
With talons of love

How will you show up?
As the gravity of worms

How will you show up?
As the lightness of wings

How will you show up?
As a basket of silence holding all the noise

How will you show up?
Beastly and beriddled

Why speak in riddles?
Would you rather we not speak at all?

How will you show up?
Heartbroken and Whole

How will we show up?
Heartbroken and Whole
Heartbroken and Whole
Heartbroken and Whole

I Bent My Ear

They were calling for attention
as I walked past–

the fruiting fungi
and horsetails whispering

mugwort and trillium
bellowing the rainbow
through the redwoods

and those baby ferns
curled up like seahorses
of the forest
confiding in me
their secret potencies

I suppose I could have kept up my pace
stepping past them

never learning what song
they were singing

or what the slug was saying
in its bright hum of the earth
from his banana mouth
and sure-footed saunter

But as they were calling
so charmingly and gently

I slowed down
and bent my ear

I had to give them
what they asked for

She Saunters Ripe With the Season

She, like moon with no pace
but that of her slow wonder,
wanders to where the brambles bend
in homage to their early yield

gifts ripe with the season, soft with promise

she puts down her titles, duties
into old mad river time
and loves herself like water

soft and flowing
sauntering like an artist

ripe with the season, soft with promise

stoops to smell the river weed
stops to feel the sun, her skin
winding her way through the day

until with gentle feet and clear heart
dusk arrives, and a crescent moon opens up

ripe with the season, soft with promise.

Persimmon

In the way summer never catches up with fall
and fall never catches winter

spring is a dream of winter
that winter never lives

In the way that each unfolds
an invisible season from within

you go up to unfold yourself
into the mountain

to paint the sky of your life persimmon
with syllables of relentless affirmation

to share some unadorned moments
with that secret silence

where the night has eyes
and the rocks breathe fathomlessly

You feel the lichen on your skin
before seeing it

arching a bare back against a granite boulder
bronzed belly sipping an autumn sun

calories you know you will need to launch again
before falling yet again into the world overflowing

Boann

I've met several River goddesses in my day, but only one visited me in human form. I talked to her just once, and never again saw her. This poem is dedicated to her.

Through a bold gate of moon she flowed
Boann the goddess, a river old
Appeared to me to talk awhile
From beyond the West with friendly smile

"I had to stop and grab your ear
You looked like someone really here"

"I really am," I had to say.
For I'd been here the entire day.

"In a world of do and do
A remnant of the Puritan view
It's so rare to really see
a person who can simply be"

I'm a simple forest poet, dear
I live beneath the laurels here
I practice listening to what I hear
And how love might conquer fear

"I thought you might, it's why I stopped
A worthier craft cannot be thought
The world needs the artist's eye
To catch the things that most pass by"

And she began to tell her tale
as I poured us both a cup of ale

"My first home was in the woods
Our bath a creek, our stove a fire
A candle was our only light
In our simple forest shire

Soon we lived by rickety wagon
That was during the world war
we lived in a hazel hut
With boughs our roof, and duff our floor"

Then she told how to build a bender
(Or wiki-up as here it's called)

Take some laurel young and tender
and plant them in a circle wide

Take the laurel stems, bend them all
and tie them at the center tall

To keep rain out, trench around
So your wiki-up is warm and sound
For the roof, hemlock's great
But other trees will do as well"

She turned to leave and walk away
but before she did she had to say,

"Eat your oats and millet grains
that'll keep you warm in winter rains

They call it dirt, but earth is clean
it's where we're from is what I mean

Both grandpas tilled the soil
farming was their bread and toil
something in my blood and bones
is rooted in the earth as home

Scratch the surface in my homeland hearth
You'll find a pagan of the earth!

I'm nearly 80, I've seen a lot
Which I try to paint, I try to pot
My craft is painting and some pottery
to try to capture what I see

A poet's voice is vital, dear
To show a world beyond the fear

To paint a world askew, anew
to fling a dream in a word or two
don't give up, the world needs you!"

At that we shared a tear or two.

"I'm Boann, she said, with a grin
For the goddess and the River Boyne
A wonderful chat it has been
I'm sure we'll meet again

Have a happy hazelnut day,"
she said as she walked away.

I, TOO, AM LARGE, CONTAINING MULTITUDES

The phrase comes from that Great Affirmer Walt Whitman, world-opener, exquisite celebrator, grand experimenter, bold ecosensualist: "Do I contradict myself? Very well, then I contradict myself, I am large, I contain multitudes."

Sectioned in four parts, this poem is an anchoring in the Great Affirmation, a bright and real caress over our multitudes. It is excessive and indulgent, and I'd like to think Whitman would have liked it.

The Great Affirmation: Well-Stretched Arms

To put my western boots on
for the lonely descent
in deepening dark

knowing it will be a long while
before the dawn will break—or if.

But also to know the strength
of my calves and limber heart
libidinous and unrestrained

To spring from these muscles
my inviolate motion
sometimes slow, sometimes quick

but sure, steady, alive!
all my incarnate days

While I can, the movement
of my savage and beautiful body, unalloyed
in bright unbridled kicks of freedom

My electromagnetic self
commingling with my analog
and mottled-leaf self,

permeable and wanting all
the worlds—oh, what storms!

To love these shoulders strong
and pulsing, pushing
to the edge
of my shadows, stretching

then flinging further
turning the wheel in new directions

To make from these soft, brown eyes
all the beauty of the world
and the unsavory truths of it too

Yes the shimmers, the hues,
patterns and spirals, the ripples
and the great green garments of summer
fading into autumnal maculations

no less the stark winters
and raging rivers of me
in their endless faces

Just as the bones hold it together
singing life as much as death
I say yes to new trees and old
to the burnt and ragged

Uncountable forms silhouetted
against the birth of day and apricot dusks
as much as the dying day
and impenetrable nights

Cliffs and clouds, petals and bubbles,
moonlight on silver ferns
laughing with the falling leaves
maroon and gold, the swooning birds

To embrace with these well-stretched arms
friends and lovers
a few enemies at times

Even the crafty stones
and unpredictable feathers,
yes, every single one of 'my' selves.

To laugh, belly and eyes
for all the joys, beauty beyond possibility
and yet it is

bringing tears to the surface
of my rough-bearded face.

But also no less, the griefs
unthinkable, unbearable, yet borne
yes, the world is too cruel and dying–
unimaginably so.

Yet also, the world is being born
in each moment,
and is too generous, too kind–
unexpectedly so.

The Great Affirmation: Glad of My Paws

Best of all to caress
play and pulse
push and pull
gather and explore

inviting all the world
with these infinite fingers

sensitive, lined and lithe
touching the surface and depth of things.

The uncountable textures
the skins, the contours,
forms and shapes,
the soft and hardness of it all.

How the stone touches back
the tips of even the wind nibble
as the ground presses back
following its promise to Earth to hold you

the slick and silky,
scaled, slimy,
bumpy, coarse, and grainy of the world–
I welcome them into me.

The sand falling between them
the rough grooves of redwood
the suave of madrone in her winter garb
the granular solidity of granite

the thin wisp of alder leaves
leaping yellow into fall
the delicate racemes of pink-flowering currants in spring

the plumping berries shouting summer!

Or the thin cylinder of her neck
eager eyelashes, whimsical wisps of hair
that won't obey, crooked drifters.

The contour of her waist,
the line from breast to holy hips
to her delicate butterflies,
the grand horizon
wet in the thick warmth of it all.

Yes, I am glad of my paws.

The Great Affirmation:
Vast Arousal

I drench myself in passions,
vast and inebriate

alloyed with all
the minerals

Oh yes all drops of things
raw and unfettered

Tasting the wild plum,
blackberries boisterous and free

Yes salt and fat,
sweet red wine and water
spicy chiles and bitter wild mustards
transmuting toxins like some fungi alchemist

I accept on my palate wide-like-Shasta,
my robust tongue
on her lips, all lips
inside and out

Yes her darkest leaf,
Yes her wettest petal
of wild sea and copper

To banish all shame
beyond the mountains,
slanted voices of others no more

My endless curiosity,
my vast arousal for, with, as the world

To greet the aromas with my premium nose:

buckeye husks, hay, cut wood and lavender,
cedar and sage as much as rose and cinnamon
pheromones and falling leaves
garlic and cut grass,
the journey-work of the stars

To have fallen in love,
to have risen in love

to have melted and mushroomed in love
to have been constellated and confused
in love

to have been poured out in love
and have been spored and shimmered in love

the unlikely comraderies
the subtle and sharp connections

to befriend the lowliest creatures
as well as those that soar

equal to me the caddisfly larvae
and falcon
the sand toads and beetles
no less than dolphin–
all seers of deepest wisdom

the unexpected grace of egret
sliding silence over my head–
like him, I am miraculous.

My exquisite ears
swimming in the symphonies
of the world:

songs and strings
and heavy beats

the raven's croak, the lightning crack
the creek, gentle and ocean, roaring
as good as my twin.

The singing and soft cries
mixed with exasperated cries

tears and guffaws for every season
from dark halls of fall
to riotous spring–
mine and yours and yours…

The Great Affirmation:
Petty Heart, Beautiful Heart

Yes my mistakes,
my habits unclean,
all my petty hooks,
unrequited desires,
indecent hungers
and narrowness of vision

My ignorance and boundless egoism,
my ungoverned impulses
flinging me into danger
as much as into joy

my not knowing and my knowing well enough
but still doing wrong

my indebtedness, my unearned privilege
my greed and uncompromising
dark devils paining the world

The grief I carry still, the grief
I caused
the inflictions on your heart,
on the water,
on the living soil,
on plants and on the animals–
Oh, I too have waged brutal wars!

But also, to hold these
with the widest wings outstretched.

To ring my bones with real flesh
from living full and if not without fear
then fear as faithful friend

yes good stomach—ample and adored
well-traveled thighs, both resting and pumping
gliding my hands, my well-worn knees and feet
through the thickets of confusion and wonder

like one who has wrestled and known gods
bringing even my loathing into warm embrace

Yes, to my manly feet
my sensitive feet
my dancer's feet
my wild feet

Sauntering past all the gates
tipping my hat to the guardsmen
with a wily grin
jumping across boulders
winking if it comes to that

walking beyond approved forms
playing footsie with water
with the trickster

with you under the table
and no one has to know

To walk the world like a madman
or like a man madly in love

To fling love unwisely
sometimes indelicately,
sometimes dazzlingly and deliciously

to throw it like thrush in ever-widening circles
of iridescent song loops —

Oh, what a beautiful heart!

THIS MESSY CELEBRATION

Savage Pulse

A savage pulse
asking of you
more than you think
you can handle
lives in here

Did you expect to love the world
and not die daily
from the sundry shocks
both sharp and subtle?

Did you expect to find
on the edge of every granite cliff
a pillow for a weary head?

A sweetness in every mouthful
bit off from the big loaf?

Surely the wintered sun
and rough and gripping tide
disabused you
of such sentimentality

Yet surely the same sun
and the lunatic arriving
of a faultless sea
taught you, Beautiful Gambler,

how a lover shows up
with an unconditional caress

But if you've yet to find
the capital C in Celebration
in the seed of each moment

strap the searchlight
around your ribs

and shuffle like a crescent moon
over all your little resistances

your feet becoming wiser
with each toe-stub in your heart

until they become sandpipers
dancing at dawn
around the fingers of the sea
knowing exactly where to go

This Messy Celebration

Where we're from we walk barefoot
in the rain.

We know what water tastes like when it's alive.

The soft rain. The hard rain. Even the mischief
rain, full of teeth and kisses.

It's a way to put our flesh
into the big memory with each drop.

A way to get clear and clobbered,
to cobble together the next right step

as we sing mud almighty
oozing with gratitude.

We know we will never turn our backs
on the sound of Earth's symphony

and what terrible things trees shout
when they burn into marmalade skies.

That Life and Death are lovers
that can never be pulled apart.

That it's a good omen
when a covey of quail comes cruising
across a permeable path
chirping up impossible questions

making of the madrone a bell tower
announcing the moon's imminent/eminent arrival.

It's our tradition to gobble it up–

it tastes nothing like vanilla

or easy dreams.

It's thicker than mud, richer than quail yolk.

We reach our rugged hands out
to feel the falling truth
in its multi-colored fingered delight.

We let ourselves become birth
and death doulas simultaneously

as the lunatic liminality
wets our winter faces facing west
or weeping.

If and when the light arrives, we know
we will have done our part

with bodies bending
becoming prayers pulsing
in this messy celebration

Trust the Shimmerings

Did you crack yourself open
at dawn

or at dusk?

Or did you slip away again?

How much beauty
must the world wash over you
for your heart to break open
onto the wet rocks?

How much for you
to reach a conclusion?

I'm talking about the shimmering

the gleam and glittering
pure press of guttural uttering
in you like the first vibration

Your footprints, where are they?

Your bellyprints and moonburnt eyeballs?

You outrageous fire, dancing, burning, licking at the world?

I'm talking about that fabulous blast
your sea-storm at last

that high savage power
blue and vital

your silver scream
on the pummelled shoreline

The beasts are far? No—the beasts are within.
What clawed out of you
at first light?

I'm talking about foraged
and furry creatures
scurrying down the stream
of your marrow

Slit your self down the middle
pull your skin to the horizon
and drip like a mountain

Come to your senses,
cum in broad daylight
body lit with love

I'm talking Big Trust
like screaming thistles
surprised at their own purpling

the dandelion bursting
through concrete

Now tell me,
will you crack yourself open
at dawn or at dusk?

Or will you slip away again?

That Hole in the Horizon

Every evening I dig a hole
in the horizon

to place what I love
and what I want to love
into it

*'Though if I want to love it,
doesn't that mean I already do?'*

Is meant to be a real question,
not an answer.

I've thrown lawless songs and dances
into that hole

and too many queries to count
should have filled it up by now

fists and furies
wounds and whys
and all my favorite fears

beautiful resistances and clingings
slough into it
with scarcely a word

Then each day
I cover it up
with the darling dregs of the day
while water rushes in

as the sun takes them all
to where all things woven
from foraged lives go

as a truce gently crawls
into every crevice of me.

Good thing there's no end
to the hole

because there's no end
to my digging.

Sirening

So you've stopped hearing
the birds and earthworms
of your soul

you've misplaced the treasure
at the bottom of your breath

If only the sirening would stop
for a moment

Whether in its bright red pouring
you imagine when that high pitch
ambles through the fog

or the sound of brutal headlines
thundering through parts of you
you have yet to catch up with

or the signals bellowing "Stop!
Your life as you knew it is over.

Prepare for an extended rendezvous
with your beautiful mistress, loss."

If only.

Then you could uncatch your breath
and wade in gently
counting the wild blessings
chirping on the shoreline

and the color of joy
in your eyes
could stretch out
under a bold sun.

Yet you already know
there are others sounds

and that to put your breath in a jar
for safe-keeping
is no way to write a life

that the only sirens worth a near-drown
are the lures of tender touches

from creatures
not meant to be shackled

So you raise your hands
to both sides of you
and pull. Pulling

each ear
until all the old lustrous melodies
funnel their way in

and the water draws up
into your torso

until the wingsong of the sea
rings true

until the critters in the soil of you
shake you free

until your inhale
and exhale
match that of Earth's

Freckle

The slightest freckle floats in
on the surprise-side of the season's face

landing in me with a new breeze
blowing through

like the Queen of Change
sovereign of the land

One I might not really recognize
until after it has turned the corner on itself

onto the next conversation
with utter unutterables

I grin in recognition,
knowing that from its soft kiss

I'll gather mountains of meaning
and make a home of it

Then, my eyes would widen
as I chuckle from inside my fifth gut
as I slow my endless doings

that try to reserve a place
at the table of belonging

Knowing a freckle is just a freckle—
yet not less than a freckle

Knowing I'll worship its ancient art,
its soft elegance

that will eventually fade into

a full-chested decay

with the invisible current
of the Queen's unbending law

Knowing the mottled-leaf of me
too will drop

and like September,
I too will take a trusting turn
towards the next season of Life

ONLY IN IT FOR THE CONVERGENCE

Tell Me, Where Do You Mark the Center?

I'm not here to catch anything
says the ditty about love
pretending to be an inkspot
of a man on an island
in a river
on the back of beetle
carrying a leaf to the other shore.

Nor to catch up on anything
or to be caught

and I try to believe it,
thinking to myself
the song knows better.

I'm just in it for the convergence.

Don't let your eyes settle
too long on these words—
amaranthine sunset
labyrinthine river bed
hyacinthine autumn
placed here just for your convenience

Hell, why NOT for convenience, that devil!?

But we're not here for the convenience.

"You're really here, aren't you?" River asks.

But it's not a question, but an observation
hidden as a question
that a different goddess made
and I wonder if they are one and same one.

Yes, I am really here.
And here. And here.

The great blue heron glides by
like a satellite silent and in orbit
around the river.

I'm in its orbit now or he in mine.
Or we in its—the Great Orbit.

Tell me, where do you mark the center?

Don't let your ears purchase it too highly
heron says again.

Sometimes you eddy, but not too long
for it feels too damn good to join the waves.

Are you just in it for the waves?

The dew on the sunglasses in the sand
that was once a mountain
once cleaned a monk's robe in Madagascar
was once farmer's urine
that became the peach in a jazz singer's
breakfast of oatmeal

THAT orbit became a song.

I'm not saying I know the song
but here we are together–
you, me, the dew, the suns and moons,
the violence and inescapable shadows
the pulpy memories of past
and future

and the great blue heron
with a song running through it all.

And maybe that was exactly
what she was singing about
in that ditty about love
and the loss of love–
I just hadn't been born yet
so how could I know?

How could I really know?

Don't Puzzle Over the Meaning

Don't puzzle over the meaning

When did the river ever stop
to ask the rock
of what it's made?

A caress will do
and it's on its way

Don't puzzle over the meaning.

A poem. A river.
The foam. The world.
A woman. A girl.
A man unfurled.

And everything between
Seen and unseen

Who know how to play.

Who knows how to play?
They're on their way.

To where we're all headed.

It's the what, not the why.
Don't ask me why.

The big-picture-map-
on-the-box-cover-trap
Been there, done that

Better make sure
it's the right box/map/trap

or make your own.

They say you are
what you puzzle over

So might as well be
a puzzle dove hovering
over the treasure trove
in your pleasure grove

so you can stand
inside both your
stone and your rivers.

Either way, abundance is unavoidable.

The Waves Know

Summer pulled itself out from under me
and slunk out to sea

slowly or suddenly
depending on whether I showed up
or not

When I belong to the moment
rather than the moment belonging to me
nothing is lost

though everything's a shapeshifter
when I've been sitting with the waves

asking about the turning
of the tide of life

finding I have more in common
with the bright green sea lettuce
than I ever knew

with the rotting algae
than I ever wanted

Let me break it down for you,
the sand bugs said.

What would it mean, the sea asked,
what would it mean to roll over
the surface of things
and roll back out again?

To keep coming back?

To touch and not take

the boulders, proud sentinels of the coast

To touch and not take
the love, that happened to grace your shores?

What would it mean
to grow your sea lungs
and dive down deeper
league by league

settling into the soul-tide
quiet depths of true voice?

There's a moon inside everyone
according to that improbable creature Rumi–
the waves know it
so why do I feign forgetting?

I never did hear Moon complain
of its imperfect reflection
on the bay

nor Water complain
of the moon's relentless here now, gone tomorrow

It's not that I wished for an easier world
it's that I get into things
like a mussel

a barnacle of love
fastening myself to rocks called dreams

when all I really want, (I lie)
is to wave
(I lie)

to tell the truth of it.

I want to be here. I want it all.

I want to float like kombu:
(the storm comes—
the storm never happened)

I want to be the barnacle,
the sun and the moon,

to be the wave
and all the tidbit poemlets
on the playa.

What if I dared to be
what the land and sea
agree to be in me?

Memoir: All the Holy Things

In the 7th grade I invented
interstellar travel
via hydrogen ion propulsion.

Combined with giant sails
that would harness the chaotic wind
from solar storms—
we could go anywhere.

Even here.

I was in the library
where the sound and scent
of old books
were background to my life.

That was back when libraries knew how to be themselves.

They were quiet and sensitive.
I was quiet and sensitive.

Since then, I haven't done much engineering.
NASA, please forgive me.

Unless you count constructing façades,
adopting them as masks of belonging.

You see, earthstorms moved in
thrashing my branches
and I did the only thing I knew
how to do:

I deployed my earthworms
and became someone else.

Clearly, who I was wasn't safe.

That was the wrong lesson.
But I knew not roots and took to riot.

I learned to be noisy and insensitive.
I learned anger gets you things.
Mostly the wrong things.

I learned, to my chagrin,
I couldn't photosynthesize,
which led me to adopt some peculiar eating
and moving habits.

I discovered walking and small talk.
I discovered cheese and liquor.
I discovered coffee and masturbation
and chasing things.

Over time, I learned to need them.

Fantastic wounds and tornadoes refined me
and my feet walked it all together
into my torso.

This continued rather inelegantly
for decades

until one season
I gave myself the gift
of walking with death
into the bottom of things.

How can I describe the down
and up of things
without mentioning love?

Oh fierce heart, I learned

to breathe, I learned
to eat like it's the first time.

I learned to honor the seasons
and all the splendid contours
of resistance

and its first-mate, acceptance.

I guess what I'm saying is
at some level
I've always known
the value of silence

that sensitivity is a gift
and who I am is a sacred mystery

that storms are essential
to the journey

That being here is one thing
but really being here
is yet another way to love

and is the path
to all the holy things.

ABOUT THE AUTHOR

Ryan Van Lenning, M.A., is author of *Re-Membering: Poems of Earth and Soul*, *From Inside These Wild Ones*, and a collection of haiku, *High-Cooing Through the Seasons*. His new collections, *Trust the Ceremony, F*ck the Ceremony, Trust the Ceremony*, *An Ambitious Silence*, and *Becoming Beautiful Barbarians* will be released throughout 2025-26. He is the 2019 recipient of Jodi Stutz Poetry Award by Toyon Literary Magazine for his poem 'All The Walls Between Them' and his poetry appears in various poetry journals and the book *A Walk with Nature: Poetic Encounters That Nourish the Soul* and *Behind the Mask: 40 Quarantine Poems from Humboldt County*. He facilitates 6-week workshops called Write Your Wild River, Earth Intimacies, and Deep Belonging in the Great Turning a couple times a year.

Ryan is Founder of Wild Nature Heart, supporting people to re-connect with the wisdom of both inner and outer wild nature, to live their callings into the world, and to assist in the work of repairing broken belonging during this collective initiation. He is a teacher, ecotherapist and wilderness rite-of-passage guide and lives among the forests and rivers of Northern California.

ABOUT WILD NATURE HEART

Wild Nature Heart supports people to connect with the wisdom of inner and outer wild nature, to embody our wholeness, and to live our wild purpose into the world in order to inhabit our particular niche in the ecosystem of healing and justice. Through 1-on-1 ecotherapy, earth-rooted mentoring, custom and group wilderness rite-of-passage ceremonies, and various Deep Belonging courses, ecospiritual workshops, and seasonal gatherings, Wild Nature Heart cultivates an ecospirituality that nourishes our deep belonging in the animate web of life in order to do the decolonial work that we are called to do in this moment of the Great Turning.

Wild Nature Heart believes that to cross this threshold into species maturity with a next-season guest pass we must keep our imaginations robust and make moves that subvert inherited paradigms of fear and supremacy. We are being invited to fall through the inherited maps into new territories towards collective liberation. As crises continue to invite us across thresholds of initiation, we crack open the paved highways of our hearts and bodies to allow the tributaries of our holy longings and wild purpose to flow in and out.

The journey is both a daily and life-long practice, as much as it is multi-generational and multi-species. We practice simultaneously being both death doulas to the world that is dying and birth doulas to the one being born.

www.wildnatureheart.com

OTHER TITLES IN THE *RE-MEMBERING SERIES*

The book that began it all:

The 75 poems in *Re-Membering* are an unabashed celebration of the sensuality of wild nature. Redwoods reach without apology towards the sky, and rivers flow with unflagging energy towards the ocean. This collection re-members Ryan's personal explorations into wild nature, but it also re-collects for all of us a time when our kinship and inter-connectedness with the natural world was self-evident, and invites us to fully re-inhabit and say "Yes!" to our sensual natures, our animal bodies, our playfulness and creativity, connection, mystery, and our instinctive love for this beautiful, sentient Earth.

"Ryan's poetry speaks deeply and clearly to the awakening to our true interconnected nature, which is the only way we can transform our world."
—Molly Young Brown, author of *Coming Back to Life: The Updated Guide to the Work That Reconnects* (co-authored with Joanna Macy), Editor of *Deep Times: A Journal of the Work That Reconnects*

From *From Inside These Wild Ones* (2025)
Book 3 in the *Re-Membering* Series

Gorgeous Storm

This gorgeous storm
keeps getting stuck in my teeth

as if I could bite-size my way
to destiny

When all I want
is to have it come
racing out my lungs

Like a waterfall plunging
over my luscious tongue

flooding all the landscapes
of my crooked life.

to join the wrens and warblers
and beloved lusts

of a wounded world
washing away the old debris

Please, Storm, please,
knock down the weak branches
of my being

Prune me for the season
I am meant to live

EXCERPTS FROM RYAN VAN LENNING'S FORTHCOMING BOOKS

From *Trust the Ceremony, F*ck the Ceremony, Trust the Ceremony* (2025)

Door-To-Mystery-Knows-Where

There is a door to Mystery-knows-where
and you are being invited to step through

The new doorway through which you pass
is framed with grander questions

where you'll pick up pieces left
in your canyons long ago

and find on the side
fragments resting by the fire

drinking ale for an evening tale
of dreams wanting to find their flesh

Put them in your wide-brim hat
and home in on your succulent belonging

becoming an obsessionate one
like a convict who loves their fate

This is the door to Mystery-knows-where
and you are being invited through

From *An Ambitious Silence* (2025)

The Silent Here of Things

I finally stood in the lush truth of it.

I never walked so slow, never inhaled
so many trees
savored so many stars.

Dawn hung around my neck
like a sigil
river stones became emblems
of radiant belonging.

Some 'I' in me had said, I can't live
like this

but some big eye in me—
I think it was an owl—replied, Yes.

Yes you can.

They just kept letting me in.

Everywhere I didn't knock.
No keys.
No doors.

The living sky my heart-home roof.

Only the silent here of things
on the back of the map
where all the real places are.

From *Becoming Beautiful Barbarians* (2025)

We are the Machine, We are the Rust.

We are the Empire and the Heart that Composts Empires.

We are the Emergency and the Inter-mergence.

We are the Lover learning to leap.

Right here in the Brambles.

Right here in the heart of the Beast.

How big can our sky be? How deep our roots?

Let's walk each other home.

www.ingramcontent.com/pod-product-compliance
Lightning Source LLC
Chambersburg PA
CBHW071725020426
42333CB00017B/2388